DESTROY YOUR STUDENT LOAN DEBT

The Step-by-Step
Plan to Pay Off Your
Student Loans Faster

ANTHONY ONEAL

RAMSEY
PRESS

Published by Ramsey Press, The Lampo Group, LLC
Franklin, Tennessee 37064

This publication is designed to provide accurate and authoritative information with regard to the subject matter covered. It is sold with the understanding that the publisher is not engaged in rendering financial, accounting, or other professional advice. If financial advice or other expert assistance is required, the services of a competent professional should be sought.

Editorial: Ara Vito, Rick Prall and Jennifer Day
Cover Design: Chris Carrico and Gretchen Hyer
Interior Design: Mandi Cofer

ISBN: 978-1-942-121-24-4

Printed in the United States of America
20 21 22 23 24 POL 5 4 3 2 1

"All things are possible with God."

—MARK 10:27

INTRODUCTION

"THIEF!"

That's what the cruel voice shouted through the phone. The debt collector's anger rang louder than the crashing waves below. Julie was sitting in her rusty sedan at her favorite spot 200 feet above the Pacific Ocean. She let the phone slip through her fingers and rested her head on the steering wheel. She was defeated. Not like when your favorite team loses the championship by one point. Like really defeated—feeling fear and helplessness and despair all at once. The kind of defeat that makes you think about driving off a cliff.

But Julie wasn't a thief. In fact, she felt like she was the one being robbed. Her student loan debt was pressing in on her from all sides. The bright, fulfilling future she once thought her college degree promised was gone. Instead, she spent her days avoiding collectors and her nights crying herself to sleep.

As Julie shared her story with me, she told me she'd fought her student loan debt for over 20 years—and it had only gotten bigger. A lot bigger. Because she wasn't able to keep up with all the payments, her balance had grown from $15,000 to over $60,000. She was desperate. Nothing she tried made a difference. Julie was out of hope—and she's not the only one.

Have you been there? Are you there now? I was there at 19 years old—homeless, living in my car, with thousands of dollars of debt. And I hear similar stories from people all over the country all of the time: "Anthony, I need help! How do I pay off my student loans? *Where do I even start?*"

The reality is, student loan debt is a massive problem for us today. Check it out:

+ There are 44 million people in the United States right now[1] paying off $1.6 trillion of student loan debt.[2]
+ A recent survey showed that most current and upcoming graduates believe they'll pay off their student loans in an average of six years. But the reality is, it takes closer to 20 years or more![3]
+ Forty-nine percent of student loan borrowers end up with higher loan balances five years after graduation! That means almost half of borrowers are actually losing ground as they struggle to pay off their loans.[4]

That's unacceptable! When you're signing on the dotted line to borrow money for school, no one thinks this is going to happen to them. No one expects to not be able to pay their loans back. But it happens all the time to people in every walk of life—from those who never graduated to folks who are now doctors and lawyers. And that's why I wrote this book. Because even if your situation looks hopeless, you need to know it's not!

The way we're taught to approach student loan debt is all wrong. If you have student loan debt, it's easy to get overwhelmed and stressed out. It's easy to look for ways to lower your monthly payments. It can even be easy to ignore your debt altogether, thinking you'll get around to it someday. But the last thing you need today is relief from your debt. What you need is to get mad at it.

No matter what you believed when you took out your loans, the reality is that if you don't get serious about getting rid of your debt fast, there's a good chance it's only going to get bigger and stay with you longer. So whether you're drowning in debt like Julie was or you don't think your student loan debt is even a problem, I'm going to show you why you need to dump your debt fast and how to do it.

Over the next hour or so, we're going to face the reality of what student loan debt is *actually* costing you—because it's probably worse than you thought. I'll also show you why you can't count on loan forgiveness and tell you when I would recommend debt consolidation (spoiler alert: it's not very often). And then I'll walk you step by step through the proven plan to pay off every dime of debt as fast as humanly possible. Along the way, we'll also hear from some amazing, hustle-and-grind people who destroyed their student loan debt and are now living lives of freedom!

Will it take some hard work and sacrifice to destroy your debt? You bet. Will it be worth it? Definitely. Just ask Julie. After we talked, she got crazy intense. She took on three jobs, sold most of her stuff, slashed her spending, and paid off that $60,000 in only 27 months. And most importantly, there's a light in her eyes now. She has hope again—and a bright future. I know you can do it too! It is possible to get yourself out of debt and take control of your life.

Take a second right now to picture yourself in the future completely free of student loan debt. What does that look like? How much extra money do you have in your bank account each month? Think about the business you want to open, the vacation you want to take, the wealth you could be building, the kids who won't have to worry about money because their parents built a legacy for them. Think about the house you want to own. Think about all the ways you could bless others by giving generously.

Now get excited, because that future is closer than you know. It's not an impossible dream—it's a reality waiting to happen. You don't have to spend decades paying off your student loans.

There's a better way. You can pay it off faster than you think—and you can start today!

PART 1: THE PROBLEM

Before we can dive into the solution, we have to take a closer look at what caused this mess. Here's the hard truth: *you've been lied to.*

As a young, college-bound student, you were told the only way to pay for college was to take out student loans. They called it "good debt" and an "investment" in your future. It was the price you had to pay for the best chance at getting a job, making good money, and pursuing your dreams. Everyone did it. But the truth is, borrowing money—for any reason—doesn't open doors for you. It slams them in your face.

You guys, it's time for some straight-up facts: There's no such thing as good debt. Debt sucks. Period. Even student loan debt.

Debt is a thief that steals the life you were created to live. How? By keeping you paying for your past instead of enjoying your present and investing in your future. Money is a tool that gives you the ability to make choices. With money, you can . . .

Buy a house
Be outrageously generous
Travel
Change careers
Get married
Start a business
Raise a family
Retire some day

If you have the money, you can do any of these things because you have *choices*.

But when you're a slave to making payments to a lender every month, you lose your ability to have choices. The money you would have used to make progress toward your goals is spent paying off your past. You end up like a hamster on a wheel—running in circles year after year and going nowhere fast.

Here's what most people don't understand: your income is your single, biggest wealth-building tool. And it's the main way you give yourself choices. If you want the power to choose how you live your life, then you need *all* of your income to work for you. Dumping your debt is the only way to reclaim your income and your life.

THE UGLY TRUTH ABOUT THE STUDENT LOAN INDUSTRY

Believe it or not, the student loan industry and its lenders are *not* on your side. They never have been. Sure, they made you think they were on your side by giving you a way to pay for college. But the lenders knew all along that once you signed that loan agreement, you'd be tied down for years while you paid everything back plus interest. A *lot* of interest. (Yeah, that part wasn't always clear.)

Let's look at a couple of examples. We're seeing an average of $35,000 in student loan debt per student at the time of graduation.[5] So let's say you have that amount of debt with monthly payments of $363 and a 10-year repayment plan. The current interest rate of an undergrad federal student loan made by the U.S. Department of Education, aka a federal Direct Loan, is about 4.5 percent (which is on the low end of interest rates for federal loans).[6]

With those numbers, you would end up paying back a total of over $43,500—that's over $8,500 in interest!

Because student loans can be really hard to pay back, a lot of students are taking more than 10 years to pay them off. If you paid off the $35,000 over a 20-year period, your monthly payment would be $222 and you'd end up paying back over $53,000. That's over $18,000 in interest! The amount you'd pay in interest alone is enough to buy a car, save for a wedding, or launch a start-up.

But let's take these numbers to the next level. Sadly, I've known plenty of students who took out over $100,000 in student loans (and actually, there are over half a million borrowers right now with over $200,000 of student loan debt).[7] If you paid off $100,000 by making monthly payments of $556 per month for 25 years, you'd end up paying back almost $167,000. That's over $66,500 in interest. Just imagine all the things you could do with $66,500.

Let me say it louder for the people in the back: interest is *no joke*. It's the way lenders make money and stay in business. But paying out all that money in interest isn't even the worst part. The worst part is that every month you spend paying back debt is another month without your freedom.

When my friend Kristin was headed to college, she was one of those students who casually signed up for student loans, believing

they would help her in the long run. She thought it was the only way to afford school. She even worked in financial aid as a grad assistant, encouraging students to apply for student loans because it was the "normal" thing to do. It wasn't until later that she realized the weight of what she'd have to pay back.

"I had no idea how much interest upped my payments until I started paying my loans," she told me. Kristin ended up paying almost $15,000 in interest alone!

After a few years spent slowly chipping away at her almost $52,000 of student loan debt, she discovered the Baby Steps (which we'll cover later on), and everything changed. Kristin followed the plan and started getting intense about paying off her loans by working crazy-long hours at her side job and cutting out a ton of expenses from her life. And in a little over 18 months she was able to pay off the final $28,699.66! *By herself!*

Here's what she said about becoming debt-free: "I love knowing that my education is officially mine now! I have financial peace, and I'm no longer a slave to the lender!" She got her income back—and her life.

And want to know something *really* cool? Now she's an elementary school counselor who's able to talk to young students and their parents about the importance of solid money habits and saving up for college in advance. Kristin is living proof that this plan works. But her story also shows just how deceptive the student loan industry can be. The idea that loans are the only way to pay for school is one of the many lies students believe, and as you can see, it makes their lives much harder in the long run.

REPAYMENT ALTERNATIVES: DON'T BELIEVE THE HYPE

Here's another lie you might have heard about student loans: go ahead and take them out now because there are a ton of ways you can get out of paying them back later. There are a couple repayment alternatives floating around that borrowers tend to put all their trust in—namely what's called *forgiveness* and *discharge*.

Forgiveness (or cancellation) is when you're not required to pay back your student loans because of your job. Discharge is when you're not required to repay your student loans because of circumstances out of your control, like your school closing. In reality, though, the odds of either of those happening are pretty slim.

Let's break these types of repayment alternatives down even more.

Student Loan Forgiveness

Of course, you've probably heard about student loan forgiveness as an easy way out when it comes to paying off your student loans. Even the term *loan forgiveness* sounds so heartwarming, like a hug for your bank account. But trust me: it's not the saving grace you're looking for.

You might think the U.S. Department of Education is rescuing you through their forgiveness programs. But the problem is, forgiveness is unpredictable and depends on where you work, how many payments you've made, and whether or not the government changes the eligibility requirements (and they're changing all the time).

Here are three of the most commonly hoped-for types of student loan forgiveness.

1. Teacher Loan Forgiveness

A lot of teachers bank on getting up to $17,500 of their federal student loans forgiven because of their line of work. But before you imagine life without that student loan payment, you need to read the fine print—and then read it again. Here are just a few examples of the requirements for this type of loan forgiveness:

+ You have to work full time as a "highly qualified" teacher for five academic years in a row (the "highly qualified" part comes with a whole other list of requirements).
+ You need to teach at a low-income school or educational service agency (which also comes with a whole other list of requirements).
+ You must have taken out the loan *before* the end of your five teaching years.
+ You need to make sure you've never had a late payment.[8]

2. Public Service Loan Forgiveness

If you're one of the lucky few who's eligible for public service loan forgiveness, you'll have to:

+ Work full time for a qualifying employer, like the government or a nonreligious nonprofit.
+ Make (or prove that you've made) on-time payments for 10 years.
+ Have federal Direct Loans.
+ Have an income-driven repayment plan (which means the amount of each monthly payment is based on your income).[9]

But like I said earlier, getting your loans forgiven with this program doesn't happen as much as you'd think. As of March 2019, 86,006 applications have been submitted for public service loan forgiveness. Out of those 86,006 applications, only 864 were actually approved and just 518 lucky people were granted student loan forgiveness.[10] That's only 0.7 percent!

Even if you were initially approved for this type of loan

forgiveness, it doesn't mean you'll actually get it. In 2017, some borrowers who qualified for the program received letters of denial after years of working toward forgiveness.[11] This means they spent 10 years in low-paying jobs, only to find out they wasted their time and effort. They could've been debt-free a lot sooner if they had just paid off their loans instead of waiting around for them to be forgiven.

3. Borrower Defense to Repayment

This type of loan forgiveness is for people whose school misled them or violated certain state laws. You only qualify if your school committed fraud related directly to your federal student loan, like claiming more graduates got jobs straight out of their program than actually did.[12] Applying for borrower defense involves a lot of legal jargon and a lot of documentation. I feel for the people who have to deal with this, especially since the qualifying rules continue to change.

Student Loan Discharge

There are a few different types of student loan discharge, including Total and Permanent Disability Discharge and Closed School Discharge.

In order to qualify to get your federal loans discharged through Total and Permanent Disability Discharge, you have to prove your disability status through Veterans Affairs, the Social Security Administration, or your physician. If your loans *do* get discharged, you'll be monitored for the next three years to make sure you really are totally and permanently disabled. If you're no longer disabled within those three years, you'll have to start making payments again.[13]

As far as Closed School Discharge goes, don't let the name

fool you: this doesn't mean all your loans automatically get forgiven if your alma mater shuts down. This only applies to people who took out loans through the William D. Ford Federal Direct Loan Program (Direct Loan), the Federal Family Education Loan Program (FFEL), or the Federal Perkins Loan Program.

Even then, you only qualify if:

+ You were still enrolled when the school closed.
+ You were on an approved leave of absence when the school closed *or*
+ You withdrew from your school, and it closed within 120 days of your withdrawal.[14]

If you want to read up on other types of forgiveness, cancellation, or discharge (plus the long list of requirements that go along with them), I recommend you check the official Federal Student Aid website.[15]

When You Can't Afford Your Monthly Payment

It's no secret that a lot of people struggle to pay back student loans. When you're stressed and money is tight, it's only normal to look for help. But don't make the mistake of thinking forbearance, deferment, or default is a solution to your problem. These options may provide emergency relief, but they won't serve you in the long run. Here's what each one means:

+ **Forbearance:** Your payment is put on hold, but the loan continues to build up interest. There are two types of forbearance: general (the lender decides your level of need) and mandatory (the lender *has* to grant forbearance based on your situation). Again, the requirements are very specific and only apply to certain types of loans, which you can learn more about at the Federal Student Aid site.[16]

+ **Deferment:** With deferment, you *temporarily* don't have to make payments, and you may not be responsible for paying interest on your loan. Not everyone is eligible for deferment or forbearance, but you might qualify if you're unemployed, serving in the military during wartime, or serving in the Peace Corps.

+ **Default:** This is what happens when you keep missing payments. Your loan is referred to as *delinquent* the day after you miss one payment. And if you continue to miss payments, you go into *default*. This means you failed to pay back the loan based on the terms you agreed to when you signed the paperwork, and it can have serious consequences. You could be taken to court, lose the chance to get other financial aid, or be required to pay the entire balance of your loan right away.[17]

Don't risk this, you guys. Forbearance, deferment, and default are where people really lose control of their student loan debt and see their balances skyrocket by tens of thousands of dollars. None of these are good options! I know when your payments are suffocating you, it can be tempting to look for a temporary quick fix. But the truth is, when you get mad enough at this debt, you can get your loans paid off faster than you think.

Consolidation and Refinancing

The other big way people think they'll find relief from student loan debt is through consolidation and refinancing. Student loan consolidation is the process of taking all of your different loan payments and turning them into one big payment. It also takes the weighted average of your interest rates on your loans and rolls them into one. And only federal loans can be consolidated for free through the government.

I *only* recommend consolidating your student loans if:

+ It doesn't cost you anything to consolidate.
+ You can get a fixed rate instead of a variable rate.
+ Your new net interest rate is lower than your current net interest rate.
+ You *don't* sign up for a longer repayment period.
+ You *don't* get so relieved by the thought of a single payment that you lose your motivation to pay off your debt fast!

Refinancing is different from consolidation in that it deals with private loans—or a combination of federal and private loans—and you have to find a private lender or company to do this for you. They will pay off your current loans and become your new lender. At that point, you'll have a new rate and new repayment terms. Again, only do this if you get a lower interest rate and there's no cost involved. Since you'd be working with a private lender in this case, there probably will be—so proceed with caution.

Now, here's what I want to warn you about: most people looking at debt consolidation and refinancing are asking the question, "How can I lower my payment to make this debt more manageable?" *But that's the wrong question.* The right question is, "How can I make a larger payment each month so I can get rid of this debt faster?"

Listen, you don't want to make your student loans more

"manageable." You want to get them out of your life *forever*. That's the only way to build a solid foundation for your future.

There's Still Hope

If you've heard anything so far, I hope it's this: don't rely on debt forgiveness, discharge, forbearance, deferment, or consolidation to magically get rid of your student loans. You don't have to jump through hoops or wait around for the government to save you. And you don't have to waste years of your life working a job you hate or holding your breath to see if you catch a break, all while racking up thousands of more dollars in interest.

Yes, the student loan industry is shady. No, you probably didn't have the complete picture when you signed that loan agreement at 17 or 18 years old. But these are still *your* loans, and you have the power to pay them off faster than you could with any standard repayment plan.

Don't wait. Don't count on anyone else to get you out of this mess—and don't let anything stand in the way of your future. You can kick these loans to the curb starting *now*, and I'm going to show you how. The bad news is that *you* are the solution—and the great news is that *you* are the solution! Me and the team at Ramsey Solutions have shown millions of people how to get out of debt and you're next. It isn't easy, but it is simple. And the best part? *It actually works.* You can do this! We are with you! Let's go!

PART 2: THE BASICS

Alright, you guys. Ramsey Solutions's proven financial plan is called the 7 Baby Steps. (And in case you're wondering—yeah,

Dave Ramsey is the "rice and beans, beans and rice" guy.) Don't panic—following this plan does *not* mean you're going to starve or that you can't pick something up in a store without Dave sneaking up behind you and yelling, "Put that back!" But if you want your life (and your money) to change, you can't keep doing what you've always done. This plan is the fastest way to pay off your loans and take control of your money instead of letting it control you! *You* are the boss of your money—not the other way around—and it's time to destroy that debt.

So, what are the 7 Baby Steps?

Baby Step 1: Save $1,000 for your starter emergency fund.

Baby Step 2: Pay off all debt (except the house) using the debt snowball.

Baby Step 3: Save 3–6 months of expenses in a fully funded emergency fund.

Baby Step 4: Invest 15% of your household income in retirement.

Baby Step 5: Save for your children's college fund.

Baby Step 6: Pay off your home early.

Baby Step 7: Build wealth and give.

If you want to know how to build lasting wealth and achieve financial peace, these are the steps. One of the reasons the Baby Steps work is because the fastest way to take control of your money is to do **one thing at a time**. You're not paying off your student loans *and* saving for the beach *and* putting away money for retirement all at the same time. You're going to focus on crushing one goal at a time—and this is the order.

Right now, we're only going to focus on Baby Steps 1 and 2. Baby Step 1 will lay a strong foundation so you're standing on solid ground. Baby Step 2 will show you how to attack and destroy all of your debt. You can think about the other five steps once you're out of debt!

BUDGET LIKE YOU'RE
THE BOSS—BECAUSE YOU ARE

I learned the hard way that you're either going to happen to your money, or your money is going to happen to you. If you want to take control of your money—if you want to accomplish *any* of the Baby Steps—then you have to learn how to make and stick to a budget. I get that you're here because of student loan debt, but if you're tempted to skip this section, don't. *Your budget is the key to destroying your debt.*

Now, don't let the word *budget* freak you out. A budget is just a plan for how you're going to spend your money. You need to have your plan in place at the beginning of every month, and you'll need to make a new plan each month. And this isn't your average budget—it needs to be a zero-based budget. (If budgeting makes you nervous, we've got your back. We created the world's best budgeting app called EveryDollar that will help you set up your budget in minutes. And, it's free!)

Zero-based budgeting is the simplest kind of budget out there. You don't have to be a math pro for this. All you really need to know is this basic equation:

$$\text{Your Income} - \text{Your Expenses} = \$0$$
(Your income minus your expenses equals zero dollars.)

Simple, right? And don't worry. The zero-based part doesn't mean you start out or end up with zero dollars in your bank account.

It means you give every dollar a job to do—whether it's for housing or food or savings or debt. You're using all of your income for *something* and putting every dollar in a spending category.

Here's how it works:

1. **List all your income for the month.** This includes paychecks and cash you make at your side hustle. List any and all money that's going to come in for the month.
2. **List your fixed expenses for the month.** These expenses include anything you know you *have* to spend money on (we call them the Four Walls): food, utilities, shelter (your mortgage or rent), and transportation.
3. **List other common monthly expenses,** like restaurants, entertainment, and clothing. Check your bank statements to get an idea of what you typically spend money on each month. Don't forget to list minimum payments on your debts (including that student loan).
4. **Subtract your total monthly expenses from your total monthly income.** The total should be—you guessed it—zero. If the total isn't zero, you either have too many expenses, you need to find a way to make more money, or you're not using every dollar of your income. Keep working your numbers until you hit zero—this is the key to zero-based budgeting.

Here's an example of a zero-based budget paying off debt in Baby Step 2. We're going to use easy, round numbers to make it simple. And keep in mind, this budget follows our teaching in *Financial Peace University*. So you'll see, for example, that giving is the first spending category and that housing is no more than 25 percent of the monthly take-home pay. More on that later.

Zero-based Budget Crushing Baby Step 2

INCOME *(This is what you take home, after taxes, each month.)*	$3,000.00
EXPENSES	
Giving	$300
Saving *(Once you hit Baby Step 2 and are attacking your debt, this is zero until you're debt-free.)*	$0
Housing	
Rent	$750
Utilities	$200
Gas/Transportation	$250
Food	
Groceries	$350
Restaurants	$0
Personal	
Cell Phone	$60
Miscellaneous/unexpected expenses	$60
Lifestyle	
Clothes	$0
Entertainment	$0
Insurance	
Car	$70
Renters	$15
Debt	
Furniture store	$60
Credit card	$60
Car loan	$140
Student loan	$360
Extra money you're throwing at debt	$325
WHAT'S LEFT TO BUDGET	$0

5. **Track your expenses throughout the month.** Once you have your budget mapped out, the last step to budgeting is to track what you spend to make sure you're not overspending. The easiest way to do that is to log how much you spend as soon as you make a purchase so you don't forget. Even if you spent 99 cents on an app, keep track of it in your budget. It all adds up.

Here are some other things to think about when it comes to budgeting:

+ **Giving is important.** When you're making your budget, don't forget about giving. When you're desperate to get out of debt, it's easy *not* to give. At Ramsey Solutions, we believe in giving away 10 percent of your income no matter which Baby Step you're on. Giving was the first category in my budget when I was digging myself out of debt, and it still is today. Putting others before yourself and giving even when you don't have much puts things in perspective. It reminds you there's a bigger purpose to your financial journey— and that God's got your back, even in the hard times.

+ **Find an accountability partner.** If you're married, you and your spouse should do your budget together so y'all are on the same page before the month starts. And if you're living the single life, find an accountability partner like a friend or family member you trust who can help you stay on track. Just make sure they believe in getting out of debt like their life depends on it, or you might lose momentum.

+ **Give yourself some time to get used to budgeting.**
  It takes most new budgeters about three months to really get the hang of it. Don't be hard on yourself if your budget is off the first month or two. Keep at it and by month three you'll be a pro!

How to Budget with an Irregular Income

If you work on commission or earn a different amount of money each paycheck, don't stress. You can still make a zero-based budget work for you. Just budget using the bare minimum you expect to earn that month, and make sure you cover the Four Walls first—food, utilities, shelter, and transportation (in that order). Then list out the rest of your expenses in order of importance. When it's finally payday, work your way down the list. If you run out of money, anything on your list you didn't get to has to wait until the next paycheck.

Remember, your number one wealth-building tool is your income. If your current job isn't giving you enough stable income to cover your expenses and dig you out of debt, you might need a bigger shovel—like adding a part-time job or finding a steady, full-time job.

The Best Way to Track Your Zero-Based Budget

To budget well, you need a plan for your money, *and* you have to track how much you're spending through the month. Some people rock the old-school vibe and do their whole budget on paper. If you like writing everything down and keeping track of all those little details, I'm seriously impressed. Other people use a spreadsheet (which is my worst nightmare). Both of these can work for sure, but they require a lot of discipline to do them right.

I'm an app guy all the way, and I love our EveryDollar

budgeting app. My favorite part is that it crunches all the numbers for you. So it's super easy to adjust your budget and move funds around whenever you need to. The other thing I really love is that keeping track of your purchases is so easy—which means you don't need a calculator every time you buy something to see how much money you have left. And because EveryDollar is an app, you get to carry your budget around with you wherever you go. So if you make a last-minute run to Target, you always know how much you can spend to stay on track.

So, here's my challenge to you: I know your phone is somewhere near you right now. Whip it out, download EveryDollar, and spend a few minutes setting up your budget. The app will walk you through how to do it. (Or do it on paper or spreadsheet—whatever works for you!) If it's not the beginning of the month right now, do it anyway. Just do your best to figure out how much you've already spent this month—looking at your bank statements or online account will help you do this! I'm serious. Creating your budget is the very first step to tackling your student loan debt.

Did you do it? No? I'll wait. . . .

Okay, are we good to go? I'm proud of you. You're one very big step closer to being debt-free!

BABY STEP 1:
A $1,000 STARTER EMERGENCY FUND

With budgeting under your belt, you're ready to start Baby Step 1! The very first thing you need to do is save up $1,000. Why? Because life is going to happen while you're attacking your debt. There are going to be unexpected expenses that come up, and you need a way to cover them without racking up any more debt on a credit card or with a personal loan.

I want you to save your starter emergency fund *fast* so you can attack your debt without losing ground. I also recommend keeping this fund in a savings account—separate from your checking account—so you don't accidentally spend it all on Starbucks. We'll talk about how to save up that $1,000 in a minute, but first we need to answer a really important question: What's an emergency fund for?

What Qualifies as an Emergency

This right here is where a lot of people trip up—because when you want something bad enough, anything can become an "emergency."

Let's talk about what an emergency is and what it isn't. Your car breaks down and you need to rent one? That's an emergency. Broke your ankle on the dance floor? Emergency. Have a date coming up and need to look as fly as possible so this person will fall for you? Not an emergency (sorry). Here are the three questions you should ask to figure out if you need to use your emergency fund or not:

1. Is it unexpected?
2. Is it necessary?
3. Is it urgent?

The more you can answer yes, the more your situation qualifies as an emergency, which means you can probably go ahead and dip into your fund. Just use your brain—stop and think about it before you access that cash. You'll know if it's a real emergency or not.

How to Build Your Starter Emergency Fund

If you already have any nonretirement savings, you want to keep $1,000 of it for your starter emergency fund and throw everything else at your debt in Baby Step 2. If the only savings you have is in a 401(k) or Roth IRA, leave that alone. You want to avoid the steep tax penalties for cashing out early. Plus, you're earning compound interest, so the longer you leave that money alone, the more it grows. Just stop contributing to any retirement accounts for now—and focus all you've got on saving $1,000 fast and getting out of debt.

If you don't have $1,000 in savings already (a lot of people don't!), use your new budget to put every cent that's not being used for basic expenses toward your emergency fund. So let's say your income for the month is $3,000, and your expenses for the month total $2,800. You'll put the last $200 toward your emergency fund. If you get to the end of the month and still have money left over in any of your budget categories, throw all of *that* at your emergency fund too!

The most important thing in Baby Step 1 is to do it *fast*. The faster you save this up, the faster you've got a cushion against life happening. If your financial situation changes, for example, and you're making more money, don't blow your raise on a phone upgrade because "you deserve it." This is not the time to treat yo'self. You can do that later. Right now, you need to hit that $1,000 mark.

Most people going through *Financial Peace University* save their $1,000 in about a month. If you're having trouble getting this $1,000 saved, you need to get creative. Pick up an extra shift at work, start a side gig, sell anything you don't need on eBay or Facebook Marketplace, or cut something out of your budget that's more of a "want" than a "need."

Don't get me wrong. I'm not against fun or date nights or nice stuff. But if you're serious about paying off your student loan debt, saving this first $1,000 needs to be your biggest priority. You don't have to sacrifice that date night, but you'll need to do it differently for a while. Just remember there are plenty of ways to have fun for little to no cash. I'll get to tips on how to make extra cash fast as well as ways to save more money in Part 3.

When $1,000 Isn't Enough

A thousand dollars will cover most emergencies you face while you're getting out of debt. But sometimes, it's just not enough. What do you do then? You have a few different options, and most of them involve some kind of negotiation and thinking outside the box.

If it's something like a big medical bill, for example, talk to the billing department at the hospital and negotiate with them. They may be able to give you an income-based discount that you can pay in full or put you on an interest-free payment plan that you can cash flow over the next few months. Pro tip: get everything in writing!

If it's something like a car issue, shop around by asking your friends for reliable mechanics and then calling each one to find the best deals. Make sure you get a quote before you authorize any work and focus only on the bare-minimum fix that will let you get around safely. The point is to do only what you *have* to do to get through the emergency and to stay focused on getting out of debt. Now isn't the time to do any extra stuff or buy things that are just nice to have.

If you have to use your emergency fund, deal with the emergency and then immediately replace that $1,000 as fast as you can. Then keep going on the Baby Steps.

Once you've got your $1,000 saved, congratulations! Now you're ready for Baby Step 2 and the debt snowball.

PART 3: THE DEBT SNOWBALL

My own Baby Steps journey went something like this: *Save $1,000 for my starter emergency fund? Boom. Got it. No problem. On to Baby Step 2. Okay, pay off all my debt (except the house) using the debt snowball? Crap.*

Baby Step 2 can feel impossible at the beginning—like there's no way you'll ever be debt-free. I know I felt that way! But it's time to face your debt head on because now you've got new tools to help you conquer it: You've got a budget that's working for you. You're disciplined in your spending. And you've got a plan. You've never been more ready.

All you need now is some momentum! Turns out the best way to make a snowball is to just start with a little bit of snow and roll it around until it gets bigger and faster. Keep doing that, and over time, it will get big enough to really do some damage. That also happens to be the best way to pay off your debt.

THE DEBT SNOWBALL

Once you have your $1,000 starter emergency fund, *stop* putting money into your emergency fund. You're now ready to move on to Baby Step 2 and destroy your debt with the debt snowball.

The debt snowball method is a debt elimination strategy where you pay off your debts starting with the smallest balance and work your way up to the largest one. Just like a real snowball, you'll gain momentum and pick up speed with every balance you pay off.

Here's how it works:

Step 1: List your debts from smallest to largest (regardless of interest rate). Make minimum payments on all your debts except the smallest one.

Step 2: Attack your smallest debt like your future depends on it (because your future *does* depend on it). Once that debt is gone, take that payment—plus any extra money you can squeeze out of your budget—and apply it to the next-smallest debt. Keep making minimum payments on the rest.

Step 3: Once that debt is gone, take its payment and apply it to the next-smallest debt. The more you pay off, the more your freed-up money grows and gets put toward the next debt. Just like a snowball rolling down a hill! Repeat until each debt is paid in full.

The Debt Snowball in Action

I'm going to assume your student loan is your biggest debt, and maybe it's your only debt (that would be great, right?). But if you're already living with one huge expense that was paid for with borrowed money, chances are you have more debt on top of student loans. I know I did. Just for fun, let's say you have four debts:

1. Furniture store loan: $600 with a $60 payment (I definitely financed some furniture when I was in college. It was a dumb idea.)

2. Credit card debt: $2,500 with a $63 payment
3. Car loan: $7,000 with a $135 payment
4. Student loan: $35,000 with a $363 payment

You've already listed these debts in order from smallest to largest—awesome. Now you can make minimum payments on everything except the furniture store debt—you're going to attack that one with a vengeance. So let's say you get real serious about bringing in some extra money (using the strategies we'll talk about next), and you end up with an additional $600 per month to put toward paying off your debt. You're on a roll!

Next, you'll take the $60 furniture payment and add it to the extra $600 you're making per month to get a total of $660, which means that whole furniture loan is toast in just one month! Yesss!

Now you have $660 that you can put toward that credit card debt. You'll pay $723 (the $63 minimum payment plus $660) each month until you pay off the $2,500 total. That will take you three and a half months, and then it's gone for good.

Next up: it's time to destroy the car loan. With the $723 you were paying on the credit card debt plus the $135 car payment, you'll have $858 to throw at the $7,000 total every month. In eight and a half months, that loan will be history and the car will be yours *for real*. You are on fire!

Finally, you're left with the goliath of a student loan—and it's about to go down. You know what to do. Add that $858 to your $363 student loan payment and start putting $1,221 toward the loan every month. At that rate, you'll pay off your entire student loan in about 28 months—that's two years and three months. *Only two years and three months!*

With the numbers we used, you'd pay off $45,100 of debt in just over three years. And that's if you have multiple debts.

It's totally possible that you could pay it off even faster if your student loan were your only debt, or if you're able to throw even more cash toward your debt over those three years. Even if you weren't able to bring in that much cash per month, you'd still pay off your debt faster with the debt snowball than you would with a 10- to 30-year repayment plan—guaranteed.

Why This Works

At this point, it's probably clear that the debt snowball isn't rocket science. It's basic math and common sense. The truth is simple like that. You might even be thinking, *Why do we need a whole book for this?* And the answer is: *because most people don't realize they can do it.* Getting out of debt fast takes determination and living with intentionality. It's only going to happen if you're willing to make some sacrifices now for a big payoff in the long run.

Way too often, people get used to having what they want when they want it, so they're not really into the whole sacrifice thing (no judgment—I've been there too). Or they've told themselves that getting out of debt is impossible, so they don't even try. Or they're just so overwhelmed and panicked that they can't see the answer to their problems is a lot closer than they think. But this stuff really works!

It works because the debt snowball is about your *behavior,* not math. We say all the time at Ramsey Solutions that winning with money is 80 percent behavior and 20 percent head knowledge, and it's totally true. Once you decide to change your behavior, something happens. The snowball starts rolling.

Momentum is actually the secret ingredient here. The adrenaline rush that comes from paying off that small debt makes you excited and hopeful that you can pay off the next one. Before you know it, you have so much money freed up from paying your smaller debts that the big one doesn't seem as intimidating anymore. The success keeps you motivated and makes you want to keep winning. I mean, let's be real. Who doesn't like to win?

My friends Alexis and Brian are right smack in the middle of Baby Step 2 right now, and they swear by the power of momentum. Their debt snowball started out at $20, and over time it's grown to $1,400!

Alexis and Brian have done a lot of the things most people do to power through their debt fast. They cut back on how often they eat out, got rid of cable, go to the library, commute to work together, and find free ways to spend time together. But they took things to a whole new level by living in a 290-square-foot tiny house! That helped them cut their living expenses even more. It's not unusual for their electric bill to be around $14 during the summer months. Sure, the tiny house life might not be for everyone, but we can all be inspired by their sacrifice and choice to live with less.

So far, since they started the Baby Steps less than two years ago, Brian and Alexis have knocked out Brian's $12,000 student loan balance and $11,000 of Alexis's student loan debt—not to mention the credit card debt and car payments they've gotten rid of on their debt-free journey.

The icing on the cake? Alexis told me that the whole process has been great for their marriage as well as their physical and mental health. Plus, they're excited about their future. "Knowing I will be able to retire comfortably and not be stressed out about it, and that we can go to Jamaica every summer if we want to—that's the kind of stuff that really keeps us going," Alexis said. I love how intense this couple is about attacking their debt with the debt snowball while staying hopeful and positive the whole time.

The Debt Snowball vs. The Debt Avalanche

You might have heard that the *debt avalanche* is another good way to pay off debt, but let me just bust that myth real quick. Besides sounding scary as heck, the debt avalanche doesn't work because it makes you focus on paying off the debt with the biggest interest rate first—which probably also happens to be your biggest debt, or at least one of the huge ones.

That might sound like it would save you money in the long run, but here's the thing: when you focus on paying off a huge debt first, it takes way longer because there's no momentum. Without momentum, you're much more likely to get discouraged and quit. You get stuck making small payments against this monster of a loan while you're still facing a bunch of other debts too. So no matter what, you feel like you can't get ahead. Is that how you want to feel while you're paying off debt? I didn't think so.

Debt Snowball FAQs

When I talk about the debt snowball, I get a lot of good questions. Let's tackle the most frequently asked here.

If I have more than one loan with the same balance, which one should I pay off first?

The rare case of having two debts in the exact same amount is the *only* time you should pay the loan with the higher interest rate first. Pretty simple, right?

If I have multiple student loans, should I consolidate them or use the debt snowball?

Remember what we went over earlier about consolidation and refinancing? Think of debt consolidation as the surface-level treatment for your money problems. The debt snowball is actually doing the serious work of knocking out your debt and helping you form good money habits. Plus, consolidation only works on a case-by-case basis. Most of the time, consolidation will result in a higher interest rate and a longer repayment term, which means you'll end up paying more money in the long run. Unless you can get a lower, fixed rate without a longer repayment term (this almost never happens), you're better off knocking out those debts one by one with the debt snowball.

What if my student loan is my only debt?

The good part about this is that you can hard-core focus on just one thing. Obviously, you won't need to do the debt snowball, but that doesn't mean it's time to kick back and chill. You'll still want to be crazy intense about bringing in as much extra money as you can every month. That way you can throw every cent of it at your debt, paying way more than the minimum monthly payment.

What do I do if something big happens to me while I'm paying off debt?

If it's a huge life event that will seriously drain your funds—like a job loss, new baby, or an engagement—this is the *rare* case when you should pause your debt snowball. Just keep making the minimum payments on your debt, focus on covering your Four Walls (remember, that's your food, utilities, shelter, and transportation), and save as much cash as possible.

For example, if you or your spouse are expecting a baby, stockpile as much cash as you can until the baby comes. If there are any complications, you'll be glad you have extra funds. Once mom and baby are home safe, you can throw whatever cash is left after medical expenses at your debt and get going on your debt snowball again.

If you get engaged while you're paying off debt, you'll want to start saving so you can cash flow the wedding (but I don't recommend combining bank accounts until *after* you tie the knot). Don't go nuts with all the wedding craziness, but do save up enough cash to avoid any additional debt. Once the wedding is over, you can start destroying debt again.

HOW TO MAKE MORE MONEY

We've talked about it briefly already, but buckle up, you guys—this is where the sacrifice comes into play. I'm not going to sugarcoat it for you: destroying your debt is going to be hard. You're going to have to go without some stuff for a while—even if you *really* want that stuff. Your lifestyle is going to have to change. By now you've realized there's just no quick and easy way to pay off your loans, and a huge part of crushing your debt as fast as possible involves making some extra money and sacrificing some of your time.

But the good news is, this season won't last forever. And if you'll get really intense about paying off your loans now, you'll be able to reap the rewards way sooner. Plus, you'll have the satisfaction of knowing that you did what everyone else told you was impossible.

So here we go. Here are some of the best ways to stack that cash!

Get Another Job (or Two or Three)

If your biggest problem is income, pick up a part-time job or side hustle on nights and weekends that can help you get that money quickly. Then, toss that cash directly at your debt. There are a ton of side-hustle options out there. Here are a few of them:

+ Drive for Uber or Lyft
+ Pet-sit or walk dogs (There's a great app called Rover that helps you find people who'll hire you to do both of those things.)
+ House-sit
+ Babysit or nanny
+ Tutor kids
+ Deliver food (through Uber Eats, Grubhub, Postmates, etc.)
+ Deliver groceries (through Instacart or Shipt)
+ Start a business selling baked goods
+ Clean and/or organize homes
+ Offer lawn care services
+ Be a personal assistant for a busy mom
+ Sell your creative products on Etsy
+ Do odd jobs, repairs, or maintenance
+ Deliver for Amazon
+ Become a photographer
+ Offer lessons or classes in something you're good at
+ Rent out your house (or a room in your house) with Airbnb

+ Be a freelance writer or proofreader if you've got the skills

+ Be a notary public (You'll need to get a license for this.)

One more option that doesn't exactly fit in the side-hustle category: ask for a raise. This one takes guts, but it could make a huge difference in your loan payments. Just make sure you've been going above and beyond in your job and helping your company win. That way, you can back up your request with straight facts about your performance. The more financial value you bring to the table, the more likely your leader will be to give a raise some serious thought.

However you choose to do it, making extra money will take a lot of determination. But trust me—it's all worth it. My friend Anna Leigh was trying to pay off $70,000 of student loan debt after graduating from college. She applied to the same company *seven times* before getting hired—all because it would give her the opportunity to make a solid income. Talk about perseverance! Once she had her full-time job, she started throwing money at her debt and then picked up two part-time jobs in the medical field. She found other ways to cut back too. She was able to save $300 a month by using back roads instead of toll roads, and

$150 a month just by getting rid of Netflix, Hulu, and Spotify.

Looking back now, she said it took a lot of extra work and often meant she couldn't go out with friends. But she's completely, 100 percent debt-free as a young professional. Anna Leigh's future is full of possibilities, and she's so glad she paid off her loans immediately instead of waiting. She said, "Honestly, the thing that helped me be successful with such large payments was doing it immediately. I never knew what it was like to have money, so I wasn't missing it once I actually got my checks. Now I feel rich!"

Her advice to other people paying off their student loans? "Listen to Dave Ramsey and *do the dang thing!*"

Sell Everything You Can

In addition to taking on new jobs, selling stuff you don't need is one of the best ways to make quick cash. Craigslist, eBay, Facebook Marketplace, and other sites are about to be your new best friends. Take an inventory of everything you own that you could possibly sell, research the retail value, and get to work taking and posting the photos online. Or you could always have a garage sale and get the whole neighborhood to join your debt-free journey.

Need some ideas? Here you go:

+ Your car (Yeah, I'm for real, especially if you've got more than one car or a huge car payment when you could be driving a cheap—but still safe—used car.)
+ Your old computer
+ Your old cell phone (Not your flip phone, though. Nobody wants that.)
+ Video games
+ DVDs and CDs
+ Clothes and accessories
+ Name-brand items (Gucci sunglasses, I'm looking at you.)
+ Jewelry

+ Furniture
+ Collectibles (like baseball cards)
+ Tools
+ Books
+ Anything vintage or antique
+ Unused gift cards
+ Toys your kids don't play with
+ Your kids (kidding)

Basically, anything in your house that's not a necessity or super special to you—and still has some sort of value—is fair game to sell.

Watch What You Eat

One of the fastest ways to save real money is to watch where and what you eat. Listen—I have *nothing* against eating out. I love it. I'm only against eating out when you're trying to pay off your loans. Just one meal at a nice restaurant can easily cost $50–75 once you factor in drinks and the tip. (And don't y'all be eating out and not tipping just to save money. If you can't afford to tip, you can't afford to eat at a restaurant!) Even quick, seemingly cheap stops at fast-food restaurants can really eat up your cash over time. Make the sacrifice now, and then you can celebrate with a five-course dinner once you're finally in the green.

In the meantime, here are some of the best ways to save money on food:

+ **Buy generic.** Name brand is pretty much always more expensive. Just look at the ingredients—you can get the exact same product for a fraction of the price if you don't get hung up on buying a certain brand. Also, for things like paper products, think about temporarily sacrificing the quality you like to cut costs even more (or use the real deal and don't buy paper plates and cups anymore).

+ **Buy in bulk.** This applies to products like toothpaste and laundry detergent that you use all the time and have to keep restocking over and over.

+ **Use everything you buy.** There's nothing worse than cleaning out your fridge and finding a bunch of expensive produce you let go to waste because you didn't feel like eating salad that week. If you buy it, use it!

+ **Meal prep.** No, this isn't just for Instagram influencers—you can do it too. If you plan your meals ahead of time and do the prep work yourself, you'll save money and time. Don't make this hard! Nail down a two-week meal plan that you can tweak and keep reusing. And don't forget to think about easy snacks to keep with you when you're on the go so you're not tempted to stop at the drive-through.

+ **Eat leftovers.** It won't kill you. Trust me—I love spaghetti leftovers.

+ **Only buy meat when it's on sale.** Meat is expensive. Buy it cheap and freeze it for later. Enough said.

+ **Don't grocery shop when you're hungry.** I can't tell you how many times I've overspent on groceries because I shopped when I was hungry and suddenly *everything* looked amazing. Trust me, that individually wrapped pickle will lose its appeal real fast once you're not hungry anymore.

+ **Try a different grocery store.** I know you love your neighborhood store because you already know where everything is. But if another store has a sale going on, it's time to get out of your comfort zone. Also consider shopping for groceries online and having them delivered to your home. There's usually a small fee associated with this, but it can curb overspending because you're only buying what you absolutely need.

Get Creative with Your Housing

You have to live somewhere—can't argue with that. And usually, housing takes up a pretty big chunk of your paycheck every month, so this is another area to seriously cut back. Your housing payment should be no more than 25 percent of your take-home pay each month (and that includes private mortgage insurance, property taxes, and insurance). I draw a hard line here because you can't win with money long term if you're paying out more than that. But when you're paying off debt, you should think about cutting back even more. Here are some ways you can do that.

+ **Move somewhere more affordable.** Yes, this one's a no-brainer. But if you're living beyond your means in an expensive apartment (or if your mortgage is through the roof), it's time to bring it down a few levels. I know moving is a hassle, but a lower housing cost will give you *serious* savings. If you have family members or friends who'd be willing to let you pay them rent so you can live with them during this temporary situation, that could be an option too.

+ **Find a roommate.** If you do rent an apartment, having a roommate (or several roommates) will cut your expenses way down. Make sure your landlord approves each roommate and that they all sign the lease so you won't be in a tight spot if one of them has to move out suddenly.

+ **Be realistic about how much space you need.** Really be honest with yourself about whether you need a big kitchen, your own bathroom, or extra closet space right now while you're trying to pay off debt. If you can get by without those extras for now and save money in the process, do it. And then later, when you're debt-free with your fully funded emergency fund in place (that's Baby Step 3), upgrade to something bigger!

+ **Look for ways to cut back on utilities.** Small steps like turning off the lights when you leave a room might not seem to make a difference, but it all adds up over time. Here's the kind of stuff I'm talking about: Check for air leaks in your home and get some weather strips if needed. Check for dripping faucets. Take shorter (and colder) showers. Use energy-saving light bulbs. Turn off the air conditioning or heat whenever possible, or buy a cheap programmable thermostat. Don't run your appliances unless they're completely full. Hand-wash some dishes (you can handle it, I promise). If you have a yard, water your grass and flower beds less. Remember, every little bit helps.

Rethink Your Transportation

Still with me? Good. I know this is a lot, but we need to find all the savings we can. Let's look at transportation next.

+ **Carpool.** What are friends for if not to carpool, am I right? Or if you like your coworkers enough, you could try organizing a carpool situation with them (who knows—they might become your real friends in the process). If you have kids, sharing the responsibility of driving to school, soccer practice, and youth group with other parents can really help with the savings.

+ **Use public transportation.** This could be anything from the bus system to subways to rideshare services. According to the American Public Transportation Association, a household can save almost $10,000 by using public transportation and having one less car.[18] Depending on how often you use public transportation, you might want to buy passes instead of individual tickets. It costs more up front, but it will help you save in the long run.

+ **Be a one-car family.** Listen, I get it. If you're married or you've got kids, having only one car can be *tough*. But remember: this is just temporary. The inconvenience can be worth it to ditch your debt faster. Think about how much you'll save every single month if you're down a car payment *and* gas *and* car insurance for that car. I have some friends who saved $650 a month by selling their second car. Their family of five was able to pay off an additional $15,000 of debt over two years with this one change alone.

Bargain Shop

When you're getting out of debt, you're only buying what you have to. But even then, you don't want to pay full price if you can help it. Here are the best ways to bargain shop:

+ **Compare prices at different stores.** It's crazy how the exact same products can be several dollars cheaper somewhere else. Research prices online before you shop!

+ **Go to thrift shops and consignment stores.** Besides being good for your wallet, thrift shopping is a blast because you can look through all the weird stuff. And you never know when you'll find a designer brand for way cheap! That goes for flea markets, yard sales, and garage sales too.

+ **Hit up the clearance aisle.** You've got to love that sale sticker. Bonus points if it shows you the original price of the item so you can feel even more like a boss. Just be sure what you're buying is a need, not a want.

+ **Use the internet to your advantage.** Don't pay full price for something if you can find it on eBay, Amazon, or Facebook Marketplace for less.

+ **Negotiate.** Don't underestimate the power of offering to pay cash for less than the asking price, and don't be afraid to walk away if the seller doesn't agree to the deal you want. Your loss of interest might change their mind.

Cut the Subscriptions and Memberships

If you love ESPN or HGTV or your foodie subscriptions, this one may hurt a little. But you're tough. You can take it. Take a look at any subscriptions or memberships you have.

+ **Cable.** Let's be honest—cable TV is a waste of time and money. There are plenty of cheaper options that'll help you avoid flipping through the channels and paying for junk that's not worth your time to watch anyway. Hulu, Netflix, Google TV, and Amazon Prime Video are all pretty affordable, but keep in mind you just need *one* streaming service at a time. Here's a crazy thought: What if you didn't watch TV at all?

+ **Gym membership.** If you're paying for a gym membership but never go to the gym, cut it. If you're going to the gym at least three times a week, I'd keep it—as long as the membership isn't overpriced. For a lot of us (me included), going to the gym helps relieve stress and keeps us sane, and you'll need that over the next few months. Individual gym memberships usually run about $60 a month. But there are cheaper options out there. Gyms like Planet Fitness cost $10-$20 a month, depending on the type of membership. There are also plenty of ways to get exercise without going to the gym—like running, hiking, playing tennis or basketball with a friend, or working out in your living room with the help of a YouTube video (your family might judge you, but that's OK).

+ **Online subscriptions.** Signing up for just one online newspaper or music service can end up costing you hundreds of dollars in the long run, especially if you originally subscribed as part of a free trial. Usually, these trials cost nothing up front, but you activate the trial by putting in your debit card information. The companies expect you to forget to cancel and then the monthly payments—which are way more expensive after the first month—will just get charged to your account. Don't risk it. And keep track of where your money's going, y'all! This is why a budget is so important.

+ **Subscription boxes.** You know those meal kit subscriptions where you pay one million dollars to have them deliver ingredients to make a recipe that you could make for way less if you bought all the ingredients yourself? Yeah, if you have one of those—time to cancel it. It's about the same cost as going out to eat, plus you still have to do the work yourself. Same with makeup subscriptions and shaving kit subscriptions and the craft kits for your kids. They're fun and might even be practical when you get out of debt, but not right now.

Go on Affordable Dates

Getting out of debt definitely doesn't mean you should sacrifice date night—that goes for married couples too. We want this debt-free process to bring you guys closer and make your relationship stronger, *not* put strain where the fun used to be. You might just have to get more creative about how you spend time together.

Here are some pretty legit, budget-friendly date ideas:

+ Have a game night
+ Watch the sunset or sunrise
+ Go to a high school or college sports game
+ Volunteer together
+ Listen to the throwback music you both grew up on
+ Test drive a fancy car (but don't buy it!)
+ Hike or walk a nature trail
+ Cook something together (even if it's ramen)
+ Find a free concert

+ Go on a bike ride
+ Check out a farmers market
+ Buy something for each other at a thrift store (as long as it's in the budget)
+ Two words: dollar menu
+ Get coffee and walk around downtown or a park
+ People-watch at the mall or another busy area
+ Make a playlist of YouTube videos and watch them together
+ Check a nearby community center for free events
+ Go to a park and stargaze (ooh, romantic)

Pro tip: if you're dating someone and they're hating on your debt-free journey or get on your back for not spending enough money on them, seriously think about if this is the person you want to be with. You guys are a team, and y'all should be supporting each other. As long as you're putting time, effort, and thought into what you're doing for your person, and as long as you genuinely enjoy being around each other, the money shouldn't matter. Plus, what's more attractive than somebody who's got their stuff together and knows their way around a budget? Put *that* on your dating profile and see what happens.

If you're already married, this is a totally different story. You and your spouse want to be on the same page when it comes to your debt-free journey. Taking a *Financial Peace University* class together can help you work through some money issues and make sure you're sharing the same vision for your finances.

Find Free Entertainment

Even if you're single and waiting to mingle until you're in a better financial spot, that doesn't mean your life needs to be one long, boring loan payment. Life while paying off debt can still be a whole lot of fun.

Here are some of the best, cheap ways to save on fun:

+ Join a book club
+ Pour into friendships
+ Listen to podcasts (They're free!)
+ Go to the library (Remember those?)
+ Start a new (inexpensive!) hobby
+ Write that book you've been thinking about
+ Learn a skill you've always wanted to learn (watch tutorials on YouTube)
+ Start a new work-out regimen
+ Find free concerts or movies in the park
+ Cook something you've never tried before
+ Check local museums and other attractions for discounts or free days

By the way, you could easily do any of those cheap date ideas I mentioned earlier on your own and still make it fun.

Use Coupons

Just the word *coupon* might make you cringe a little bit, but you guys—there's no shame in cutting out coupons, and every single cent does help. Be on the lookout for coupons in the newspaper, in catalogs, or in grocery store ads. Plus, there are plenty of other options that don't even involve scissors. Apps like Groupon and Yelp can help you find all kinds of deals. Word to the wise, though: don't go out and buy something just because you have a coupon for it. Only use the coupon if you actually need the item and it's something you would have bought anyway.

Steer Clear of Money Traps

Most of this is common sense, but I'm going to say it anyway: watch out for scams designed to trick people into giving up their hard-earned money. You have to be alert! Scams can be poison to someone who's trying to get out of debt, because you're more likely to fall for something when you're desperate for a way out. Let's take a look at some of the biggest money traps I've seen people fall into:

+ **Time-shares.** This is when multiple people buy into a vacation home for the right to use it for a certain amount of time every year, and it's a straight-up con game. Timeshares have no investment value, plus you can't give them away and they're almost impossible to sell. Stay away!

+ **Payday loans.** Ugh, I hate these things. Payday lenders offer quick cash that comes with huge fees and interest rates of almost 400 percent.[19]

+ **Surprise contest "winnings."** I know it's exciting when you get a notice saying you won a $500 gift card, but just don't go there. Watch out for emails saying you won a contest if you never entered one. And if any contest asks you to pay a fee in order to claim your prize, it's a sure sign of a scam.

+ **Investment scams.** If you get a phone call from someone giving you unsolicited investment advice or pressuring you to invest in something "right now" so you don't "miss out," hang up.

+ **Student loan-related texts and emails.** I've known people who've gotten texts and emails saying their student loans are prequalified for forgiveness, or their loan payment is due *immediately*. Do not call or text back, not even to say "stop." If anyone ever tries to tell you that a payment of any kind is due right away or else you'll get fined and asks for your payment info, it's probably phishing. Don't click on any links, and contact your lender separately to see if there really is an issue.

+ **Credit cards.** Don't even get me started on those dumb reward points, y'all. The perks like cash back, airline miles, and free pizzas (that's the one that got me, as much as I hate to admit it) are all strategies to get people to sign up and rack up debt. Instead of using debt to get airline miles, how about you just . . . save up for a plane ticket? That way, you won't have to deal with hidden fees or ridiculous interest rates.

I know all of this advice and lifestyle change sounds like a lot of work, but I promise you it all pays off in the long run. Here's another real-life example. My friends Melissa and Murphy had $229,000 of debt—$152,000 of that was student loan debt. Just the minimum payments on their student loans alone were between $450 and $600 each month. That's insane! And that's what drove them to discover the Baby Steps and start crushing their debt. Here's how they did it:

We worked a lot of overtime, made sales commissions, and Murphy drove for Uber and Lyft, which was our

47

main side hustle. We also sold items that we didn't need on Facebook Marketplace. Each paycheck we would budget for the necessities and throw the remaining cash to the current debt that we were working on destroying while paying the minimum payments on all of our other debts. We made many sacrifices along the way: We didn't take fancy summer vacations or go out to dinner all the time (we learned to cook at home). We sold one car and commuted together, and started using a new word in our vocabulary—*no!*

Are you guys seeing a theme? Get used to the word *no* because it's a big part of the Baby Step 2 journey. What makes it all worth it? For Melissa and Murphy, it was two things: remembering *why* they were doing it and imagining their lives without any payments. They wanted a better future for their children—one where their kids weren't exposed to parents fighting about money all the time. And one where they could actually build wealth, leave a legacy for their family, and get to give like no one else. Becoming debt-free was exhausting and even lonely, but any time they got discouraged they'd think about their *why* and the debt-free future they were building.

And when they saw their $229,000 of debt go all the way down to zero, the feeling of victory was unreal. "When you're in it, sometimes it feels like it will never end," Melissa said. "But we're here to tell you that you will get through it. You were created to live a life of freedom! Keep going—your efforts will pay off for many years to come!"

Did you catch that? This can be your story too! If you're having a hard time seeing just how quickly you can be debt-free, check out the free Student Loan Payoff Calculator on my site anthonyoneal.com/resources. It will show you exactly how fast you can pay off your loans and become debt-free!

GET AFTER IT!

Y'all might feel like I've been preaching at you since you picked up this book. And I won't lie—I *am* passionate about this stuff. But I'm passionate because I've been where you are right now. I hate student loans and the way they steal from your future. And I'm fired up because I know this plan works—and I know you can do it. Sometimes you just need someone to give you a kick in the butt (it's done in love, okay?).

I know that none of what I've talked about sounds *fun.* But here's what's really fun: Breaking up with Sallie Mae and making the last payment on your student loans. Paying cash for a plane ticket to go see your family because you can afford to do that now. Using your funds to bless someone in need. Knowing your kids won't make the same mistakes you made with money.

All of that is *really* fun. It's more than fun. It's serious life-change.

So before you get started on your debt-free journey, here are some tips for staying motivated while you're in the middle of the difficult stuff:

+ **Remember your vision.** Just like Melissa and Murphy told us, you have to keep remembering *why* you want to pay off your loans in the first place. Looking at the bigger picture will keep you going strong.

49

+ **Stay mad at your debt.** You hate debt. Debt is holding you back from achieving your dreams. You want to punch debt in the face. (You get the idea.) If you need some help getting really mad, check out the *Borrowed Future* podcast from Ramsey Solutions. You can find it on daveramsey.com, Apple Podcasts, Google Podcasts, or Spotify.

+ **Write down your goals** and keep them where you can see them. Or use a fun visual tracker to log your progress!

+ **Find your squad.** It can be so rewarding to make friends with people who are going through the same thing you are. Taking a *Financial Peace University* class is a great way to meet others who are just starting out on their debt-free journey. And you can always hop on over to my Instagram (@anthonyoneal) or the Ramsey Baby Steps Community on Facebook if you need some extra motivation and support!

+ **Quit comparing.** Speaking of Instagram . . . while you're on there, don't compare your story to anybody else's. Focus on *your* goals, not what anyone else is doing. And remember that no one's life is perfect.

+ **Celebrate the small wins.** Anytime you hit a milestone, do something fun or get yourself some ice cream (put it in the budget, though, okay?). Celebrating along the way will remind you that there's hope and a light at the end of the tunnel.

+ **Find success stories.** Hearing about how other people have tried—and succeeded—at paying off their student loan debt just proves the point that it *is* possible, and you can do it too! Follow others on social media who have already completed their debt-free journey. You can also check out *The Dave Ramsey Show* YouTube channel to see people from all over the country share their stories and celebrate their victories by yelling "I'm debt-free!" live at our headquarters and on the air.

I'll leave you with one last story—and this one is crazy, y'all. Together, my friends Joseph and Kayla had a whole bunch of student loan debt from undergraduate and graduate school. A total of $233,955 to be exact. They wanted that burden gone, so they got on board with the Baby Steps plan and started attacking their debt. They made a list of all their student loans—17 in total—and put it up on their wall where they could see it.

Then they went to the best place you can go when you're in debt: to *work*. Kayla said,

> My husband and I each had a full-time job plus five other part-time jobs. In a typical month we would have 4–5 days off together. We would work 40-ish hours at our full-time jobs, then add 16–20 more hours at a part-time job on the weekend. My husband would also come home on some weekdays and head to another job.

That's a lot of work! But they were determined. They just kept paying off those loans in order from smallest to largest. Their debt snowball kept rolling, and because they didn't have time to spend money, they were able to gain a ton of momentum.

So much momentum that they ended up paying off every cent of their loans in just *25 months*.

Freedom!

So keep in mind as you're reading and considering some deep and weird sacrifices that they're only for a little while. If you will go crazy creating income and cutting expenses for a short period of time, you can be free forever. The Bible says, No discipline seems pleasant at the time but it yields a harvest of righteousness (Hebrews 12:11).

Kayla said, "We were hopeful about our future when we were paying down our debt, but we're so much more hopeful now. We have more time with family and friends, and we're able to give more. It's made all those sacrifices worth it." That's what Baby Step 2 is all about!

Now it's your turn—it's time for you to take back your future. And guess what? Because you just read this book, you're one step closer to winning this game.

You: 1. Student loans: 0.

Do all the hard stuff now so later on down the road, you can live in complete freedom from debt and help others in a big way. I say it all the time: the caliber of your future will be determined by the choices you make right now. So make some good ones.

Get out there and make it happen—and don't give up!

NOTES

1. "Quarterly Report on Household Debt and Credit," Federal Reserve Bank of New York, February 2018, https://www.newyorkfed.org /medialibrary/interactives/householdcredit/data/xls/sl_update_2018 .xlsx.

2. "Consumer Credit Outstanding," Board of Governors of the Federal Reserve System, February 7, 2020, https://www. federalreserve.gov/releases/g19/HIST/cc_hist_memo _levels.html.

3. Abigail Hess, "College grads expect to pay off student debt in 6 years—this is how long it will actually take," *CNBC*, May 23, 2019, https://www.cnbc.com/2019/05/23/cengage-how-long-it-takes-college -grads-to-pay-off-student-debt.html.

4. Zack Friedman, "Wait, My Student Loan Balance Went Up After 5 Years?" *Forbes*, February 10, 2020, https://www.forbes.com /sites/zackfriedman/2020/02/10/student-loans-balance-increase /#ccfb6a946259.

5. Matt Tatham, "Student Loan Debt Climbs to $1.4 Trillion in 2019," Experian, July 24, 2019, https://www.experian.com/blogs /ask-experian/state-of-student-loan-debt/.

6. "Understand how interest is calculated and what fees are associated with your federal student loan," Federal Student Aid, https://student aid.gov/understand-aid/types/loans/interest-rates.

7. "2018 Student Loan Update," Federal Reserve Bank of New York, https://www.newyorkfed.org/medialibrary/interactives/household credit/data/xls/sl_update_2018.xlsx.

8. "Wondering whether you can get your federal student loans forgiven for your service as a teacher?" Federal Student Aid, https://student aid.gov/manage-loans/forgiveness-cancellation/teacher.

9. "Public Service Loan Forgiveness (PSLF)," Federal Student Aid, https://studentaid.gov/manage-loans/forgiveness-cancellation /public-service.

10. "Public Service Loan Forgiveness Data," Federal Student Aid, https://studentaid.gov/data-center/student/loan-forgiveness /pslf-data.

11. Stacy Cowley, "Student Loan Forgiveness Program Approal Letters May Be Invalid, Education Dept. Says," *The New York Times*, March 30, 2017, https://www.nytimes.com/2017/03/30/business/student-loan-forgiveness-program-lawsuit.html?action=click&module=RelatedCoverage&pgtype=Article&region=Footer.

12. "For Corinthian Students Who Believe They Were Victims of Fraud or Other Violations of State Law," Federal Student Aid, https://studentaid.gov/announcements-events/corinthian#fraud-violations-state-law.

13. "If you're totally and permanently disabled . . . ," Federal Student Aid, https://studentaid.gov/manage-loans/forgiveness-cancellation/disability-discharge.

14. "If your school closes while you're enrolled or soon after you withdraw . . . ," Federal Student Aid, https://studentaid.gov/manage-loans/forgiveness-cancellation/closed-school.

15. Federal Student Aid, https://studentaid.gov.

16. "Student loan forbearance allows you to temporarily stop making payments," Federal Student Aid, https://studentaid.gov/manage-loans/lower-payments/get-temporary-relief/forbearance.

17. "Student Loan Delinquency and Default," Federal Student Aid, https://studentaid.gov/manage-loans/default.

18. "Public Transportation Facts," American Public Transportation Association, https://www.apta.com/news-publications/public-transportation-facts/.

19. "What is a payday loan?" Consumer Financial Protection Bureau, June 2, 2017, https://www.consumerfinance.gov/ask-cfpb/what-is-a-payday-loan-en-1567/.

ABOUT THE AUTHOR

Anthony ONeal was deep in debt and homeless at age 19. But after hitting rock bottom, he turned his life around and committed to helping students find and pursue their dreams. Since 2003, Anthony has helped hundreds of thousands of people make smart decisions with their money, relationships, and education. He's a #1 national bestselling author and travels the country spreading his encouraging message to help students and young adults start their lives off right and people of all ages succeed with money.